Dr Ruth Gertmos

With much respect

Peter Hoy

ISBN: 979-8-6217216-8-8

Written by Peter Hayward

Design and Illustration by The Big Red Illustration Agency

Illustrations produced by: 'Milligan' of The Big Red Illustration Agency
www.bigredillustrationagency.com

Foreword

A pair of penguins known as Pen and Gwyn lived in Antarctica. Pen was an inquisitive penguin and had made friends with one of the men who, like the others, was a research scientist there to study the continent.

For most of his life Pen had studied and envied the birds in his Antarctica home. Yes, penguins flew under the sea and were masters of their skill but that wasn't the same as flying in the air like the birds.

As Pen grew older he started to map out in his mind how he could fly.

One day Pen was wandering around the men's site and noticed they were packing to go home. After they had gone Pen saw that a workshop door hadn't been shut properly. This meant to Pen's inquisitive brain that he had a workshop to himself all winter long.

Pen jumped up into the workshop shutting the door behind him,

"Wow, it's AMAZING!"

The room was full of shelves, cupboards and tools, Pen was in heaven.

Pen started to wander around the workshop touching, feeling, weighing, mentally working out what he needed to achieve flight.

He must show this to his friend Gwyn. Carefully shutting the door behind him he looked around to see if any of the other penguins had seen him. No, it seemed he was safe, everyone was at dinner.

He found Gwyn and took her to see his find. Looking carefully around Pen opened the workshop door and ushered Gwyn in.

"Wow!" cried Gwyn, "Just look at it all. I've no idea what it all is or does but WOW!"

Glue

"I know what some of it does because I spent a lot of time making friends with the man, making him believe I was his pet, so I had the chance to see what each tool did. Trouble is they are rather big and very heavy.

The other problem was the height of the work bench as we penguins are rather small compared to a man. However as I spent so much time as a pet, my man set up a pair of steps so that I could sit or stand at bench height and watch the man work."

Pen noticed a pair of wings that were part of a model the man had been making in his spare time. The wings were twice the length of his flippers and half the width again. The man normally locked the model away so Pen hadn't seen it before. He couldn't believe his luck!

All he had to do was figure out a way of attaching the wings to his flippers and he might fly. The more he thought it through, the more he felt something wasn't right. Something was definitely missing. Perhaps if he had some fish it might come to him. Penguins thought better on a full stomach.

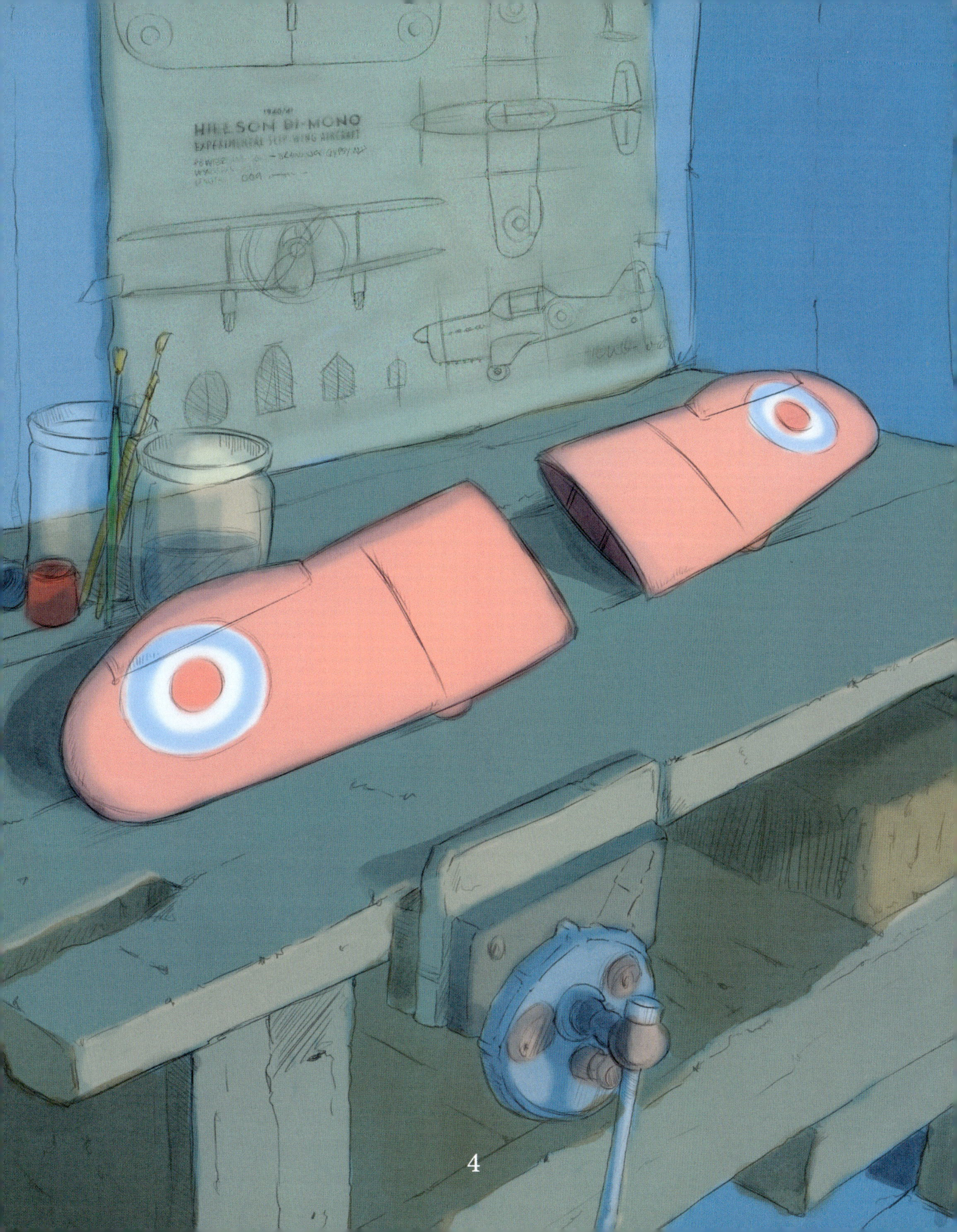
HILLSON BI-MONO

So he sent his partner Gwyn for a fish take away. While she was gone he sat pondering about flight when a sudden a gust of wind blew the door open and his thoughts were shattered by the screeching birds. That's it! Birds have wings, wings have feathers.

"We need feathers!" he shouted.

As he jumped out of the door he met Gwyn coming back.

"Feathers, we need feathers!" he called out to Gwyn. "We need feathers, grab a bucket and follow me...Come on!"

Pen and Gwyn ran and slid as fast as they could towards the nesting birds and started collecting discarded feathers, and sometimes not so discarded feathers.

This obviously did not please the birds who flew screeching, screaming and pecking after the daring duo.

Ignoring the pecking and butting of the angry birds Pen and Gwyn carried on and eventually filled the buckets they were carrying and, with feathers flying everywhere, ran and slid back to the sheds.

Breathless they closed the door of the workshop behind them and started with the pot of glue and brush to stick the stolen feathers onto the wings.

Quite a few hours later, two very tired penguins flopped back and gazed admiringly at the finished wings.

"Are they really going to make you fly Pen?" asked Gwyn, admiring their handy-work.

"Of course!" cried Pen. "I am going to be the first penguin to fly."

"After a fish supper?" joked Gwyn.

"Agreed," said Pen, "I'm starving."

After a very tasty fish supper the duo searched around the workshop for a rope, light enough and strong enough to stop Pen flying away should he fly and a gust of wind take him.

“Ah! Here we are,” cried Pen pulling some very light but strong twine.

“We’ll need to ask some of the others to help us as the wind is very strong today,” suggested Gwyn.

“Agree,” said Pen. “Let’s go and find them.”

Pen strapped on the wings and they ran and slid to the slope to where the other penguins were gathered.

"Listen," said Gwyn, "Pen is going to try flying with the new wings he has made and needs some help. We need some of you to hold this cord and stop him flying away."

"This we have to see," muttered some of the crowd.

"Never happen," said others.

"Oh come on let's hold his cord and have a good laugh when he crashes," said others.

Pen walked up the slope and the wind snatched his new wings which were well fixed to his flippers.

I'm glad I'm tied to this rope, he thought as a sudden gust pulled at his wings, taking him off the ice and into the air.

"He's flying, he's actually flying!!" called out the crowd, as the line holding Pen tightened.

Pen moved his flippers making his wings take him higher.

“I’m flying, I’m actually flying!” cried Pen, as the earth and crowds grew further away below him.

“Hold tight!” cried Gwyn, “Don’t let go of him.”

The crowd became so fascinated with Pen climbing higher in the sky that they forgot to hold on to the rope. Pen suddenly found himself flying loose and instead of being frightened, felt excited and decided to test out his new wings. He had to be the very first penguin to fly and certainly the first to fly this high.

Pen gazed down at the scene below him. The ice flows and penguins were getting smaller as he flew higher. How was he going to get down, the rope wasn't holding him any more and his wings seemed to have a mind of their own?

"Gwyn," he called out, "how do I get down?"

"Try folding your wings nearer your body, that way the air will have nothing to lift."

Without thinking, Pen brought the wings in closer to his body and immediately began to drop.

"This is not good, not good at all!" cried Pen.

Pen found himself falling. The crowd of watching penguins gasped and cried in alarm as Pen rapidly started to lose height.

"Open your wings," cried Gwyn, "start flapping like the birds do. Hurry or you'll crash!!"

Pen flapped furiously and much to his and everybody else's surprise he started to rise. His fear started to go and he actually found he was enjoying himself. He flapped harder and rose further.

"Careful, don't over do it. A little at a time," called Gwyn.

Pen was now becoming somewhat over confident. He wanted more of this flying. He wondered why penguins hadn't flown before. Flying was wonderful!

He could see further than he'd ever seen before. Beneath him the penguins grew smaller and in the sea the Orca whales looked far less threatening. They did look puzzled though, *how do you catch a penguin that is flying like a bird?*

He was free! Pen flapped harder and found that he could turn by dropping one wing, just like the birds did.

"I have control. I feel free and wonderful," shouted Pen.

By this time the crowd of penguins and seals were becoming restless. Some wanted a go at this flying and some wanted to get back to fishing and swimming, and dodging the attentions of the whales.

"Come down, please?" cried out Gwyn, "Please before you crash."

"Let him crash," muttered some of the crowd.

Pen decided it would be more sensible to come down now and try again tomorrow, the light would be gone soon.

A jubilant and very excited Pen finally touched down. He was immediately surrounded by a mob of very noisy and excited penguins, all shouting to be heard.

“What’s it like up there, what can you see? What did it feel like? Weren’t you scared, you looked so high? Can we try?”

“One at a time, one at a time, when I’ve had practice I can teach you.”

The next morning Pen was up bright and early enjoying a very nice fish breakfast.

He looked at the clear blue sky and thought this is the day. Pen and Gwyn gathered up the rope and wings, and together they went to Highpoint which overlooked the sea.

Pen fitted the wings and decided he didn’t need the rope, he would just jump off. He ran up the slope, took off and with his wings supporting him, took flight. The feeling was wonderful.

Everyone watched enviously, he would be famous, no other penguin had ever flown before. Many books have been written about it but nobody had ever actually done it.

Pen stopped day dreaming when the thermal that was giving him lift suddenly side stepped and stopped giving him lift. He was dropping at an alarming rate.

Below him he noticed one of the people's ships covered with passengers staring in awe at what looked like a penguin flying over head. He was rushing toward the ship at an alarming rate.

Having watched the birds slow down he turned the wings sideways and felt himself slowing down. Dipping one way he flew round the ship. This impressed the people on the ship enormously and they waved and cheered on Pen.

Cameras appeared, shutters clicked and pictures were uploaded to social media.

Photos and videos of him were being sent around the world, he would be famous.

But he couldn't stay up forever so beak dipping, he glided home.

When he arrived he was greeted by a wildly vocal group of fellow penguins, even the seals and walruses woke up!

Pen welcomed the praise and glowed with pride.

"I know what we must do Gwyn," said Pen, "we must make wings for you, we must both fly and share adventures as we always do."

"Me, fly?" said Gwyn, "No way."

"Yes of course, we are a team."

Gwyn agreed reluctantly.

"Let's go to the hut and make you some wings before the men come back and lock the door." Outwardly Gwyn showed reluctance but inwardly she glowed with the thought that she too was going to fly.

In the hut Pen set to work and many hours later Gwyn was trying on her wings.

"Come on", cried Pen, "let's fly!"

"Oh, oh, oh, oh!" cried Gwyn, "What have I agreed to?"

But Pen's enthusiasm was infectious and Gwyn found herself swept along up to the top of the icy slope.

"Right", said Pen to Gwyn, as he made sure her wings were on securely, "let's fly!"

Gwyn followed Pen down the slope and, with eyes tight shut, took off.

"Do everything I do", cried Pen.

"I daren't open my eyes", said Gwyn, "I'm too scared."

"Don't be silly", said Pen, "you'll get into more trouble if you keep your eyes shut."

"Okay I'll try." Gwyn opened her eyes and was amazed by what she saw. Tens of thousands of penguins clustered together watching in awe the antics of Pen and Gwyn as they flew around the sky.

"Do you have enough lift to look over that rise?" asked Pen. "I really don't have enough training or confidence."

"Maybe, after some more practice," replied an increasingly nervous Gwyn.

"I agree," said Pen.

"Good idea," said Gwyn, "after a good fish supper."

After a few days practicing they took to the skies and looked at the rise again.

“Let’s try, I’ve always wondered what was there.”

“Well, there’s only one way to find out,” said an increasingly brave Gwyn.

They both dipped beaks and started to pick up speed, then soared over the rise.

“What is that? Who is that? asked Pen and Gwyn together.

“Let’s circle round and see more.”

They banked and looked at the scene below.

Down below some twenty or so penguins were marching towards them.

“Let’s go down and meet them and see what they want,” suggested Pen.

The two took off and flew down to meet the newcomers.

“Hello,” said our two, “where are you going?”

“To meet you it would seem. We heard about your flying and would like you to teach us how to do it.”

“From achieving flight to flight school in a week,” laughed Gwyn.

Pen said, “it’s a tall order but we are happy to try.”

“We were lucky our people have gone away and left a workshop unlocked,” Pen explained.

“Why don’t you join us for supper and we can talk it over? Perhaps a flight school is not such a bad idea.”

The End

Author Biography

Peter Hayward

Pen and Gwyn first arrived in 1997 and stayed as cartoons for fun for approximately 2 years. Several reject slips later we agreed to take a break. It wasn't until 2017 that they came back and this time decided to stay.

I was a Chiropodist enjoying my work and not giving much thought to retiring, when in 2016 I was diagnosed with Parkinson's disease and forced to retire the following year.

Pen and Gwyn provide a fun distraction when the disease decides to 'play up'.

This book is the first of two, hopefully taking you, the reader, along with our duo as they turn their newly discovered flying skills into enjoyable adventures.

A donation from each sale will go to Parkinson's UK, to ensure the search for better treatments and a cure continues.

Parkinson's UK: 0808 800 0303

Printed in Poland
by Amazon Fulfillment
Poland Sp. z o.o., Wrocław

62773376R00019